In Which

Denise Duhamel

Rattle | *Studio City, California* | 2024

In Which
Copyright © 2024 by Denise Duhamel

All rights reserved

Layout and design by Timothy Green

Cover art by Michelle Weinberg
"Day for Night" (2017)
gouache, acrylic, latex on paper
30" × 44" (diptych)
www.michelleweinberg.com

ISBN: 978-1-931307-59-8

First edition

Rattle Foundation
12411 Ventura Blvd
Studio City, CA 91604
www.rattle.com

The Rattle Foundation is an independent 501(c)3 non-profit, whose mission is to promote the practice of poetry, and which is not affiliated with any other organization. All poems are works of the imagination. While the perceptions and insights are based on the author's experience, no reference to any real person is intended or should be inferred.

CONTENTS

In Which

Self-Portrait in Which I Am Not Polite

I'm not wearing lipstick. Hell, I haven't even
brushed my teeth. My nails are unpolished, ragged,
dangerous if you try to take my hand. I don't know
how else to say it … *I just don't care.* There's sleep
in my eyes, the gooey kind, dandruff on my scalp.
I have given up on deodorant and soap.
Say hello at your own peril. Sneer and I will whack
you, possibly throw an old stiletto—so duck!
I cut the line, honk my horn, chew with a full mouth,
then burp. The piercings in my ear lobes have closed,
my heart has closed. And my clothes? I've stopped
doing laundry. I've stopped the tedium of handwashing
my delicates. I've given up on bras. They hurt.
I've given up on doing dishes, smiling, shaving
(or crossing) my legs. I've given up on purses,
bangles on my wrist, any expectations of femininity.
No, you cannot sit here. No, I don't have a minute.
I've given up on the color pink and mirrors.
I leave splats on the floor and dust on the shelf.
I've never felt more like myself.

Poem in Which I Have Read the Terms and Conditions

I've checked the box acknowledging that, whatever happens,
it won't be your fault—that my insurance policy will cover
everything, except what actually breaks, that you are not responsible
for any data corruption, any mistakes in my bloodwork results,
that your mammogram can only detect so much. I know
you are not responsible for the brakes in my car, the asbestos
that might have crawled into my lungs, whatever germs
your germ killer can't kill, the long o's of my moaning
if I get sick. You can't possibly be responsible for the contents
in an envelope you send my way, any viruses or spyware
that may injure me. I understand there may be disruptions
and I shouldn't complain. I understand there may be shipping delays,
stolen packages from my porch, and that's, of course,
not your fault. You can't be held liable for damage, direct
or indirect, consequential or incidental. What you sell me
comes "AS IS" and I will deal with that. I understand
wars or "acts of God" have nothing to do with you,
that there is no such thing as "perfect" and you never claimed
to be. Of course you reserve the right to cancel my order
due to product availability. I understand you cannot—
and do not—guarantee the accuracy or completeness
of any product images or description of services. I understand
prices may go up—you need to make a buck. I understand
that you are not responsible for typos or omissions,
that, heck, you can terminate this agreement at any time
without notice. I understand that your help desk
is not required to help me and that your "chat" button
doesn't necessarily mean someone is there to talk.
I understand you may use cookies and pop-up ads—
that's all fine and dandy with me. I have waived my rights
to sue should you cause me inconvenience or harm.
It only makes sense that you can't be blamed
for the shenanigans of any third-party vendors.

I get it—you can sell my information to anyone you want
and I won't get a cut. Needless to say, you are taking
reasonable steps to protect my identifying info,
but shit happens and, hey, what are you going to do?
I, in turn, will do nothing as I have no recourse.
I understand I am consulting you at my own risk
and I, alone, am responsible for keeping myself safe.
I agree that my password has an "!" and a jumble
of letters that will be hard for me to remember.
I agree to refrain from any abusive, pornographic,
and obscene behavior and that you will determine
what those behaviors might be. Should I have a lack
of enjoyment, that cannot possibly be your fault—
enjoyment is subjective after all. I respect that your brand
is *your* brand and I will never try to copy it.
I agree that I will never scan, probe, or test
your vulnerability. I will not "deep-link," "page-scrape,"
"robot," or "spider" you. I also attest that I, myself, am not
a bot. I see the traffic lights in the squares you post and I am
checking those boxes too. Naturally, you have the right
to use my poems and my likeness in your promotions.
You have a right to take from me whatever you want.
I agree to all these terms and conditions. I know
this constitutes a legally binding agreement. Furthermore,
I understand you may post supplemental terms
and conditions at any time and for any damn reason.

Poem in Which I Married Young and Stayed in My Hometown

I never became a poet because, well, who has time?
It was a kiddish, indulgent dream—I know that now.
Each morning I read The Academy of American Poets'
poem-a-day in my inbox, and honestly, I only understand
about a third of them. I hate pretense and obscure
mythology almost as much as I hated being married.
I was a restless bride and soon started catting around.
My husband divorced me when other wives called me
the town slut. But in their whispers I heard a tinge
of envy. I let my husband have the kids. I know—
what kind of mother does that? A mother
who thought she wanted to be a poet. A mother
who thought she had big pronouncements to make.
My journals were full of scribbles about life
and my longings. I even had a few verses published
and learned the hard way poets don't make
any money. So I went to school for cosmetology
and opened my very own beauty parlor called
Her Kind, named after the Anne Sexton poem.
I poured my ambition into gel manicures, eyebrow
threading, waxing and highlights. What, you might ask,
were the highlights of my life? Transforming brides
and their wedding parties on early mornings,
right in their homes, my assistant with mimosas
and the spray tan machine. Most townspeople
have forgotten or forgiven my own transgressions.
I can make the ugliest woman feel beautiful, move her
to tears. The way a poem sometimes still moves me.

Poem in Which I Am a Cartoon Character

I am a bright pink blob with long eyelashes
but no genitalia. When a part of me falls off,
I'm whole by the next scene. My squeaky voice
annoys parents, but toddlers get a kick out of me.
My name is Denise Peace and in every episode
I try to mend broken friendships by asking
feuding cartoon characters to see both sides.
I mediate between a dog and cat who in the end
see eye to eye. I get purple parents to accept
their yellow child. I help the do-gooders
convince corporate polluters to go green.
I'm namby-pamby to the max. The little ones
love my fuchsia cheeriness but get bored
with me by first grade. Some kids even regret
liking me in the first place and pull the threads
off the plush doll made in my likeness. They retire
their Denise Peace merchandise—sippy cups
and picture books a mainstay of yard sales.
Making peace is stupid, for sissies, they say.
Or *it works in cartoons but not in real life.*
Middle schoolers despise me, deny they ever
watched my show. They call me fat and wonder
why I have no tits, why I am always naked,
and how, for fuck's sake, I could be so naïve.

Poem in Which I Never Stopped Drinking

I'm dead by now—car crash or bad fall. Or I'm still here, but feeling dead inside, yelling at Target cashiers or maybe staying home, my Tower Vodka delivered by Total Wine. I have more cringy stories or stories swirling about me. I might have slept with a student by now or a dean who's a drunk like me. I might have been fired, actually, claiming my dismissal was all someone else's fault. I never developed the good habit of flossing daily or trying to get eight hours of sleep in a row. I might have drowned in a pool or the ocean or a bathtub. I might have pissed myself in public. I have surely forgotten the rent check, credit card payment, lost my voter ID. I might have stopped writing poems entirely, with excuses about why they are stupid. I might have stopped reading them too. Or there I was, until I wasn't—a high-functioning, lampshade-wearing jokester who tripped on a step and hit her head, who tore through that stop sign on her way home.

Poem in Which I'm an Urban Planner Like My High School Aptitude Test Predicted

Disappointed I wasn't deemed a future rockstar
or supermodel, I looked at my results, having no idea
what the job description would entail. I walked
home from school on Elder Ballou Road
wishing there were sidewalks, cars winding
and whizzing as I jumped on lawns
to get out of the way. I hated the smell
of the incinerator which burned trash everyday
at 4 pm, my eyes watering. Cold Spring Park
needed more benches for the oldies and swings
for the kids. The spinner was so rusty
those who slashed their fingers wound up
getting tetanus shots. Polluted Social Pond
gave me an ear infection. Too many bars.
Too many donut shops. We needed a book store!
An art movie house! What were we going to do
with all those empty textile mills, their cold
smokestacks and brick facades?
                              Now I'm meeting
with other industry experts to work it all out.

Poem in Which I Binge

It took me a while to hear
the term "binge watching"
without flinching, remembering
my binge eating
on East Fifth Street—Cheese
Doodles or corn muffins—
whatever was plentiful
and on sale at the bodega.
I'd wash it all down
with Diet A&W Cream Soda—
two-liter bottles, always
discounted and dusty
on a back shelf—then open
the bathroom window,
no matter how cold,
and throw it all up
before my roommate Anne
came home. I'd scrub
my face and say *no thanks*
when she asked
if I wanted pizza for dinner.
We were grad students,
too poor to have a TV,
no place to put it anyway
in that cramped one bedroom
where the leaky radiator
hissed at me in disappointment.
I slept in the living room,
no door, just a beaded curtain
separating me from the kitchen,
food wrappers shoved
into the bottom of my backpack.
Sometimes Anne and I went out
to the Pyramid or Limelight,
dancing wildly, where I hoped

to lose weight. Sometimes
we'd play Scrabble and I'd score
a bingo. But after a binge
I'd tell her I had to do homework
or grade papers written by my own
students. There was no such thing
as a streaming service back then,
but sometimes I'd watch
myself from the ceiling,
leaving my body entirely
as I pretended to read,
deep breathing
minty mouthwash
and trying to ignore
the delicious smell of her slices
from Ray's. *I can't believe*
you have such discipline,
Anne laughed. *Look at me*
always pigging out.

Poem in Which I Start Out
on a Blanket in the Sand

I was never the 97-pound weakling, yet whenever I lie
on a beach blanket I panic that some jock will kick
sand in my face. I remember the ads for Charles Atlas
and his "Dynamic-Tension" program that bulked up
a skinny lad after he's humiliated in front of his fickle
girlfriend in her frilly bikini. I'm not afraid of losing
the girl, but rather my pink Yeti. I'm afraid of being
robbed, I guess, of my sandwich. How vulnerable I am
at the foot level of everyone else, when I make eye contact
with a seagull. Too many movies kill people
with "sand neckties"—and even the comedies
make me queasy. In *Creepshow*, Leslie Nielson's character
buries Ted Danson's character, leaving only his head
above the beach so that he'll drown in hightide.
As the audience laughed, I ran out of the theater
into the street. Maybe lying on the sand is too close
to lying atop a grave, a trick of quicksand ready
to swallow me whole. So I drag myself to a lounge chair
and sit up straight to watch a romance where no one
gets hurt, the unafraid waves lifting their skirts,
their white petticoats flirting with the shore.

Poem in Which I Pursued My Dream of Doing Stand-up

When articles I read in 1980 demanded
a woman comic make fun of her appearance,
I went for it. I embraced my fat because John Waters
thought fat was hilarious. In fact, I ate so much
I doubled my size and wore small, unflattering
T-shirts to highlight my stomach rolls. I wasn't afraid
to be raunchy or gross. I even farted
on stage, becoming a caricature of everything ugly
I dreaded inside me. I teased my frizzy hair to make it
even frizzier. I took my cues from Joan Rivers
and Phyllis Diller—*On my honeymoon I put on*
a peekaboo blouse. My husband peeked and booed.
I tried to repel men as much as possible
with my awesome, non-conforming physicality.
I didn't care if I embarrassed my family.
I didn't care anymore about diets or dates.
I ate whole cakes and didn't even think
about throwing them up. I went to late night
open mics, wisecracking through the jeers and booing
until audiences got used to me. I took their abuse,
gave it right back. I wore down the drunks and soon
they were laughing, even snorting sometimes.
Though still controversial, I was on the cover
of *Paper* and *Ms.* while *The Golden Girls*
made its TV debut. By the time Roseanne Barr
came around, I'd already taken up all the space
in that roly-poly lane. I let her open for me anyway.
At the end of each of my Comedy Central specials,
I would invite her back into the spotlight
and we'd bump our humongous bellies.
Roseanne grew bored. She was a deep thinker,
growing more profound with each gig.
When Jane Austen came back in vogue

[...]

17

with the movies *Clueless* and *Sense and Sensibility*,
I started my own production company
and hired so many women—even skinny
pretty comics, ones I never imagined
could break through. My wide ass opened wide
doors for everyone. Finally I had boyfriends,
handsome and loyal and attracted to my big fat
bank account. But by the time Beyoncé reunited
with Destiny's Child for the Super Bowl halftime,
my overeating and slovenly ways caught up
with me. When I had bypass surgery and lost
two hundred pounds, I knew my career in comedy
was over. Fans called me a traitor and my latest
boyfriend lost interest too—no more drunken parties
and freezers stocked with Häagen-Dazs
and Tombstone pizzas. I had to pivot so I straightened
my hair and changed my name to give myself
a second act. Roseanne had just won the Pulitzer
for her verse. I put my efforts into becoming a minor poet.

Poem in Which I Try to Be Social

I hope you have enjoyed this poem!
For others, click on the links below.
I do my best to pound rhyme and rhythm
into this algorithm. I'm so grateful
for the community we are growing together.
Please like and share and leave comments.
Sometimes I read them and put your pithy quips
in future verse. And if you are fond of
what you're reading, don't forget to subscribe.

Poem in Which My Speaker Is Bored with My Real Life

My speaker wants to make some big pronouncements, fly
with extended metaphors. She's disgusted when I toss
the coffee grounds in the trash without even trying
to make an image. Don't they look like loam,
the crushed beans once whole—yes, crushed and used,
the way I sometimes feel? My speaker wants to know
where the trash ultimately goes. Reminds me
about Thoreau—*I can stand as remote from myself*
as from another. I have long loved the way the poet
Ai's name was pronounced "I," but my speaker is bored—
I have written about this before. My speaker
wants me to be someone else in this poem—Dumbo
or Marilyn Monroe, or catapult back to my younger self,
a little girl wrapped in victimhood or a Superman's cape
depending on the day. I tell my speaker the old joke
about the naive bride—First the aisle, then the altar.
Then her hymn—I'll alter him. *Hear the "I" in aisle?* I ask.
But my speaker is unimpressed. *Aye aye aye aye,*
I am the Frito Bandito, I used to sing with my sister.
The first "aye" sounded like "I" and then
the next three sounded like they began with a "y."
A Frito bandito robbed people of their chips
at gunpoint. He was a mascot of our youth. Back then,
we weren't afraid of banditos or guns. They were just
cartoons. We weren't outraged by any Mexican stereotypes
as we would be now. I could have never predicted
the gun violence so prevalent in my adulthood,
a recent mass shooting right on the beach
where I walk every day. A 15-year-old boy
who the medics thought was hit in the heart,
his left side torn open by bullets, lived. He had
a congenital condition that placed his heart
on the right side. Can there really be a feel-good story

about a mass shooting? I think not. And yet
how giddy I was to hear this. I imagined
the shocked medic wondering at the magic
of this young man still breathing. Brig, a fiction student,
said I could use his image—*the fluorescent light of lies.*
He meant the ceilings of hospitals and the false promises
of enthusiastic doctors and nurses. He recently lost
his young wife. I, my mother. *This boy will live,* I told Brig.
This boy will live. The coffee bean unground, become whole
in reverse. This boy's heart intact. I had walked
the same beach only hours earlier. I walk it almost every day,
my speaker wanting me to make big pronouncements—
today about violence, but most days about the dying sea.

Poem in Which I Drowned
as a Six-Year-Old

The teenage lifeguard called in sick. My parents
were busy eating their clam cakes on a bench.
When I sank to the pool's bottom, no one
noticed. My little sister splashed on the concrete step
and thereafter became an only child. I overshadowed
her, giving her nightmares. My parents
never forgave themselves, even though
they had both warned a bratty me to stay
in the shallow end. I became their angel,
visited their dreams with my tiny wings.
I never went through puberty, never grew up
to write my first sonnet commemorating
my near-death, never made it to my sixties
so I could write this poem. My poor living sister,
the rule follower, now alone, would have
given anything to see me dragged out,
given mouth-to-mouth, then grounded—
no bike, no TV—for the rest of the month.

Poem in Which I Contemplate Impostor Syndrome

Each fall I have the same dream.
I'm writing on the board, my students
raising their hands, ready to answer
my questions when there's a knock
on the classroom door. *You don't teach
here anymore*, two men in suits (deans?)
tell me. *You never graduated high school—*
you still have one more intermediate
math class to take. Therefore your college
degrees are also revoked. Hand over the chalk.
I'm escorted out of Academic One,
my students laughing cruelly or maybe
nervously, feeling stung. If this could
happen to me, what about them?

Poem in Which I Have Doubts and Then Some Faith

Hardly anyone reads anymore—books, I mean. I'm at the beach
and there is only one woman (a little older than I am)
with a paperback in hand. Some people are looking
at their phones—texts, Pinterest, Bumble, who knows?
I remember not so long ago seeing shiny issues of *Vogue*,
beach books (romance and thrillers), self-help, true crime. True,
I was always the only one under an umbrella with a chapbook
or literary magazine, as I am today. Still, all those pages
curling in the breeze! What joy! Now, it's all about earbuds,
though the Rubik's Cube has made a comeback, two tweens
racing to finish the puzzle. My sister tells me there are tutorials
on YouTube where kids learn the moves. Now a group
of twentysomethings are blasting the Spice Girls' "Viva Forever,"
Do you still remember how we used to be? And that old
music video is in my head—a giant Rubik's Cube
into which a child disappears. I never solved
a Rubik's Cube back when I had one. I finished books instead,
even ones I didn't particularly like. I'd forge through
to the end as though on some rigorous moral quest.
I also finished most of the poems I started writing,
wrestling with them even when they were so bad
I ultimately forced them through my shredder. I worry
about the future of books—selfishly—
because I write them. More people read Instagram
than bestsellers and my students have their favorite Instapoets.
The word sounds to me like instant coffee. Yucky Sanka
by the spoonful in a temp office where I once worked.
But even instant coffee is coming back. Starbucks
Pike Place "Via Instant" in individual packets like the Pixy Stix
of my youth. So why do I keep writing books? Maybe
hoping they'll come back in fashion? My friend Campbell says
poets will be remembered, if they'll be remembered at all, by one

or two poems at the most. What if I haven't written
that memorable poem yet? I suppose I could post everything
online like Bill Knott did towards the end. I'm obsessing
about books but what I'm really worried about
are the dying seas, the king tides, the loggerhead
nests which I've done nothing to protect
unless signing petitions and writing poems count
and I know they don't. Have I wasted my life
in a James Wright poetry hammock? And what did I expect
would happen? Someone would read one of my books and…
and what? There's a woman with arm tattoos holding a Kindle.
Okay. So now there are three of us with reading material
on this crowded Florida beach. DeSantis wants to ban books
even though he just wrote one. My friend Michael says
I should try to get banned—have DeSantis make an example
of me to sell more copies—but these days banning seems
dire. Plus who's to say people would even buy my book?
More likely they'd just read an excerpt on *HuffPost*
and then write a mean comment. I myself have transitioned
today from reading to writing this poem in my notebook. I wonder
if any people on the beach with better eyesight than I have
are trolling people on their phones right now. Or maybe
they are keying in poems of their own? How will I ever know?
Should I roam from blanket to lounge chair and ask,
microphone in hand, "What are you reading?" "What
are you writing?" I don't have a microphone in my tote
and surely people would feel intruded upon. I know
I would, if approached, close my notebook and say,
"Me? I wasn't writing anything really," the wall
of my imaginative privacy gone, the spell broken.
Now that same group of twentysomethings is blasting Outcast.
Shake it, shake it…None of these kids could possibly remember
the Polaroid I had, the white Swinger that hung from my wrist.
It took me forever to decide what to shoot as the film
was so expensive. I can still see the TV commercial—cool
twentysomethings at the beach taking pictures of their friends.
No one had yet turned the lens on themselves. Polaroid went under
when it refused to stop making cameras. A neighbor

[…]

of my parents, who worked for the company, told them,
"Phones will never replace quality cameras." Am I holding on to books?
The idea of books? The idea of reading? I mean, reading
actual pages. Or even reading a room. When did reading someone
become like roasting them, an insult? The kids at the beach today
must be listening to what are oldies to them. Now
it's The Pussycat Dolls. *Don't cha wish your girlfriend*
was a freak like me? They're taking selfies
in their bucket hats, posing with a red bag of Doritos.
I suppose I'm a freak with my love of books, my love of poems,
my love of the planet and its creatures. A low-flying plane
rumbles above with the banner YOUR MESSAGE HERE
and an 800 number. We all look to the sky disappointed, once again
language used only to sell us something. Then I see a toddler
with *The Pout-Pout Fish*, a board book propped in the sand
next to his pail and shovel. Eminem raps over Dido's song—
It reminds me that it's not so bad, it's not so bad.

Poem in Which I Contemplate Loneliness Through a Peephole

Through my door's
magic eye I see a couple
fighting in miniature. Am I
wrong to enjoy this scene through
my one-way lens, gloating I am not either
one of them? They yell, framed by a circle,
like the end of an old Looney Tunes
cartoon. Then the ping of the
elevator—That's all folks!—
and they disappear.

Poem in Which I Invite Melodrama

I'm shoveling toxic waste with other post-menopausal women.
(Yes, once upon a time I read *The Handmaid's Tale* and watched
the Hulu series too. In fact, the crew was filming the last two episodes
of its fifth season when *Roe v. Wade* was overturned.)
But then there was no more cable, only state TV. I was caught
smuggling teas that would bring on periods—even if/especially if
my young friends thought they were pregnant. I had a safe
full of condoms and expired birth control pills and used
my online minister credentials to perform marriages for lesbians
and gay men. All my money would have been transferred
to my husband's or father's name, but since I am not married
and my father has passed, my accounts disappeared
into a government fund. I am completely "unloved"
according to the state. I lost my teaching job when colleges closed
themselves to women. All my poetry books—the ones I wrote,
the ones I read—have been burned. The resistance we put up
didn't work. All the sisterhood I so believed in fell apart.
The guards put a hood over my head when they transported me
with all the other useless old ladies. We try to help each other
with our arthritis, our carpal tunnel, our sciatic backs,
but all our meds have been confiscated and we are forbidden
to talk. Just a kind smile between us is cause for a whack
from men so young they could be our grandsons. Sometimes
they rape us for laughs. Sometimes they tell us how ugly we are.
We sleep on the ground, our ankles chained to each other
though there is nowhere to escape in this version of America.

Poem in Which I Realize What I Have Taken for Granted

free speech   lifejackets   tap water   planes
seeds   safety for children   that the STOP sign meant something
electricity   Wi-Fi   a flushing toilet   your understanding
mail delivery   laws   bank accounts   FEMA
my ability to get my way at least sometimes
phone service   my fridge   covers for my bed   my bed
my hands   my feet   my eyesight   ice cream floats   parade floats
dental floss   that somebody cared   the breeze
the air   breathable air   doctors   prescriptions   grocery stores
free samples at Costco   freedom from tyranny
my rights   my writing   my right to privacy

Poem in Which I Press Fast Forward

my young mother becomes my dead mother
my new car becomes a clunker

my blond hair becomes gray,
my favorite sweater, a rag

my beloved becomes my enemy
my enemy, someone I can't remember

my past becomes a murky place except for a few sharp excerpts
my memory, a torn plastic bag, groceries spilling onto the pavement

my love of apples becomes a metaphor
my love of apples becomes my love of applesauce

my flat chest becomes a set of breasts that later flop
my bright pink scar becomes a faded white line

my childhood friend becomes a stranger, then a corpse
my childhood home becomes someone else's home

my baby fat becomes adult fat
my new sneakers, worn and ready for Goodwill

my obsessions become ash
my fire, a cold sandwich

my scribbles becomes more scribbles
my wedding dress, a punchline

my glass of wine becomes my rewind
my beer stein, a pencil cup

my garbage becomes landfill
your trees, my kitchen table

my biggest problems dissolve
then bubble up years later like Alka-Seltzer

my belly laugh becomes a bellyache
my aversion to conflict becomes a migraine

my frown becomes a ray of frown lines
my dance moves becomes a skeleton rolled into an anatomy classroom

my childhood love of the sea becomes my adult political quest
my pet peeves soften into petty concerns then become peace lilies

my fall from grace becomes my saving
my savings become my coffin's down payment

Poem in Which Nick Helps Me Conjure More "In Which" Poems

When I tell him I'm working on "in which" poems,
imagining alternative lives for myself,
my grandnephew Nick lights up—
What about a poem in which you are a dog?
Then you wouldn't really write poetry at all
just bark out some syllables about the sublime
smell of the grass or other dogs' butts
or maybe you'd scratch out the lines in dirt with your paw
for the poodles and collies to find—since they could read "dog"
and you could write "dog"—though we humans wouldn't get it.
My dog Ringo may be writing poems for all I know
when he digs in the yard. Or maybe he howls spoken word
at Danny the mailman.
                        What if you were an only child
and my grandmother had never been born and it was just you
getting all the toys? But then I suppose I wouldn't be here
because Grandma wouldn't have given birth to my mother
who gave birth to me and my brothers. Wait—I wouldn't have
cousins either if Grandma had never been born
because then Auntie Kate would have never been born
and, most importantly, I couldn't give you any more ideas
for poems.
                    What if you were made out of Legos instead
of hair and bones, plastic primary colors, wearing Lego earrings
and Lego necklaces, with a Lego birdfeeder and Lego flowers
in front of your Lego castle? Imagining myself
not quite animal or human reminds me of a joke
which is not really a joke. *Why did the gingerbread man*
feel queasy looking at the gingerbread house? Answer:
Because it was made of his skin. Nick thinks this is funny
but not. As we try deconstruct why, we realize it's not
really a kid's joke or an adult joke, just a kind of uncanny
observation, nothing like the "dad riddles" his father
finds on the internet at breakfast. I tell Nick

I had a husband with his same name before he was born—
I've heard of him, Nick says, just the way he's heard
of my dad who died before he was born, before his mother
married. I tell him my own grandmother, his great-
great-grandmother was born in 1900 so I always
knew her age just by knowing the year.
Nick has no memories of the 1900s, which sound
like olden times to him—TVs with knobs to change
just a few channels and big ugly telephones
stuck to the wall.
                    Or what if you were born a boy?
You might be better at basketball and you'd definitely make
more money.
                    What if you lived in a world in which dinosaurs
were still alive? Would they be our mode of transportation?
Would we ride a Triceratops's back on a giant saddle?
Could we even coexist with the likes of a Tyrannosaurus rex
or would it stomp on us? Or eat us? And what about those
tiny dinosaurs, Yulong minis, only as big as chickens?
Would they become our pets instead of cats? This reminds me
of "*Feonix*/(Mystical Creature)," a sculpture I saw
at Art Basel in Miami just a few weeks before. I show
Nick the picture of it I took on my cell.
Enrique Gomez de Molina used the remains of dead
animals and birds—beetle wings, peacock feathers,
goat skin, a resin stork bill, Macaw feathers, and pig ears
to make a gorgeous 3D leaping beast that looked
as though it might spring from the wall. *And what if*
you weren't born on Earth? What if you were born
on Mars instead? You'd be a Martian and maybe
I'd be a Martian too.
                    Did you ever wonder—What if poetry
wasn't ever invented? What if poetry wasn't even a thing?
Then what? What would you do? Maybe you'd live on a boat
and your job would be to take people snorkeling.
                              What if
we lived under a mean king? Or a benevolent king?

[...]

*Or what if Burger King was the only kind of food in the world
and there were no vegetables or fruit left? We'd feel lethargic
and full all the time, right?*

         *What if you owned
your very own company? What if you were powerful
and important, like Elon Musk or Grandpa?*
Or

        *What if you were an organic
farmer? What if you sold those purple carrots? What if your
carrots were so delicious you became a millionairess?
Then I could work for you. I love digging in the dirt.*

Self-Portrait in Which I Refuse to Take Responsibility

That's me not voting because I am sick
of being lied to, me tossing my Coke Zero can
out the car window—let Coke clean up the planet.
That's me not saying sorry. That's me
not picking up your socks or mothering you
so you'll feel better about your temper.
That's me not paying my taxes and not bringing
my cloth tote to the store. That's me refusing
to wear my seatbelt, my perpetual smile. That's me
eating a pink steak, running up a credit card
I'll never pay. That's me calling in sick—so sick
of being lied to I burn down a perfectly nice house.

Poem in Which I Break My Promises

I won't be going to the party after all. And there's no way
I'm going to love you and cherish you for life. I'm gobbling the plums,
guzzling the last beer in the fridge. Yes, I'm drinking again.
I'm not going to read my students' papers. I'm not going to
upload any end-of-semester grades. I buried the promise necklace
you gave me deep in the sand for someone else to find.
I'm not a fan of telling the truth when I take the stand.
My "pinkie swear" has turned into a "screw you." I ignore
the unspoken expectations of friendship and, if challenged,
will deny I ever understood them. I'm tearing up
the promissory note, all my contracts. Promise Butter
didn't keep its promise of being a healthy alternative. Politicians
don't keep their promises, so why should I? I lied
when I said I believed in the promise of the American Dream.
All my halfhearted promises to God? I made them
under duress. The Promised Land is in foreclosure
as far as I can tell. And all those "maybes" of mine?
I hope you know I meant "no." My fingers are permanently
crossed behind my back. Did you really think I'd die
and leave you my estate? Ha! I have changed my will.
I'm leaving everything, my dear, to chance.

ACKNOWLEDGMENTS

Grateful acknowledgment to the editors and staff of the following magazines where these poems first appeared:

Agni: "Poem in Which I Try to Be Social" and "Poem in Which I Have Doubts and Then Some Faith"

Anacapa Review: "Poem in Which I Married Young and Stayed in My Hometown"

B O D Y: "Self-Portrait in Which I Am Not Polite" and "Self-Portrait in Which I Refuse to Take Responsibility"

Cherry Tree: "Poem in Which I Start Out on a Blanket in the Sand"

Conduit: "Poem in Which I Break My Promises"

Had: "Poem in Which Nick Helps Me Conjure More 'In Which' Poems"

Limp Wrist: "Poem in Which I Invite Melodrama"

The Massachusetts Review: "Poem in Which I Have Read the Terms and Conditions"

Only Poems: "Poem in Which I'm an Urban Planner Like My High School Aptitude Test Predicted," "Poem in Which My Speaker Is Bored with My Real Life," and "Poem in Which I Drowned as a Six-Year-Old"

Rhino: "Poem in Which I Am a Cartoon Character"

Tab: "Poem in Which I Contemplate Loneliness Through a Peephole," and "Poem in Which I Contemplate Impostor Syndrome"

Under a Warm Green Linden: "Poem in Which I Realize What I Have Taken for Granted"

"Self-Portrait in Which I Am Not Polite" and "Self-Portrait in Which I Refuse to Take Responsibility" were inspired by Emily Carr's essay "Another World Is Not Only Possible, She Is on Her Way on a Quiet Day I Can Hear Her Breathing," *American Poetry Review* (Volume 51, No. 3, May/June 2022).

ABOUT THE RATTLE CHAPBOOK SERIES

The Rattle Chapbook Series publishes and distributes a chapbook to all of *Rattle*'s print subscribers along with each quarterly issue of the magazine. Most selections are made through the annual Rattle Chapbook Prize competition (deadline: January 15th). For more information, and to order other chapbooks from the series, visit our website.

www.**R a t t l e**.com/*chapbooks*